BY THE STILL WATERS
Peace in the Process

Copyright © 2017
Dr. Marilyn "M.E." Porter

ISBN: 13: 978-0-9991837-4-8
10: 0-9991837-4-5

LIBRARY OF CONGRESS NUMBER: 2017917792

All Rights Reserved.
No portion of this publication may be reproduced, stored in any electronic system, or transmitted in any form or by any means (electronic, mechanical, photocopy, recording, or otherwise) without written permission from the publisher. Brief quotations may be used in literary reviews.

Scripture quotes are used by permission from Zondervan via Biblegateway.com.

SBG Media Group
Dr. M.E. Porter
thescatterbrainedgenius@gmail.com

BY THE STILL WATERS

DEDICATION

I dedicate the words written in these pages to all those who have not known the peace of still waters. I pray that God will draw you nearer to His divine peace and that you would begin to rest in the stillness of His presence. I speak it to be so!

ACKNOWLEGEMENTS

God The Father
God The Son
God The Holy Spirit

FOREWORD

Some might find it unconventional that the person listed as the visionary author, would also pen the foreword - well the blessing of being the visionary is the freedom to decide to do things differently. I am reminded of the movie "Coming to America" starring Eddie Murphy - as the prince of Zumunda and James Earl Jones as his father the King. The prince did not desire to follow the tradition of arranged marriage - while his father the King refused to accept a new way. I recall the scene when the king spoke these words to his wife, "This is the way it has always been, and so who am I to change it?" The queen very rapidly replies, "You are the king, aren't you?" In that moment a shift occurred - the king had forgotten his own power to make progress and change. With the full realization of my power to do things differently that it may have previously been done I sit to pen this foreword and prepare you to enter the pages of the magnificence of my fellow authors. I will not pen a story, or a lesson in these pages, my assignment here is not to tell my story but to build a platform for the story of others to be told and it is my great honor to host the women of God that you will meet as you begin to turn the pages.

There are many books on the market at this moment that will tell you all about the woes of life - many of them are written by Christians, for other Christians to read - but it appears the world has begun to better job at uplifting and encouraging people. There are self-help books that add more value to the lives of saints than faith-based, Christ-centered words. "By The Still Waters - Peace in the Process" is my God given role to bring the glory of God's peace back into the forefront of the minds of His people. Peace is something that we all take for granted but it is the perhaps the most needed realm of human existence after love. Jesus left us peace with us - Holy Spirit is our peace.

Life is the process of living and it can be a bumping ride sometimes but the peace of still waters is always available to you and me. My pray is quite simply that you would come to know the peace of still waters through the word of God and the testimonies of the divinely chose authors of this book.

Dr. M.E. Porter

Pastor Genae Kulah

Genae "The Destiny Designer" Kulah is an ordained prophetic minister, founder of The Word 4 H.E.R. (Healed, Empowered, and Restored) ministry, empowerment coach, and bestselling author. She has received her Bachelor of Science in Biblical Studies and Business Administration, as well as certification as a church and discipleship consultant. Pastor Kulah is an associate pastor for the Soul Restoration Center and the Ambassador trainer for the Pink Pulpit Crusade International, under the direction of Apostle Dr. Marilyn Porter.

God's Goodness as Revealed by His Name
The Lord IS My Shephard

"Giving a name entails a certain kind of relationship; it opens the possibility up of, indeed admits a desire for, a certain intimacy in relationship. A relationship without a name inevitably means some distance, naming is necessary for closeness. Naming makes true communication and encounter possible."
(Dictionary of Old Testament & Exegesis, Vol. 4 pg. 1297)

Most of us have come to a point in our lives where we want to fulfill the destiny God has for each of us. We want to know what our purpose is and how we go about achieving it. We no longer want to work according to the status quo. We know that there is more out there, and we want it. But before we can achieve the designed destiny for our lives, we must first KNOW the one who designed the destiny for us.

As Christians, we are quick to say that we love God, but do we really know the God that we say we love? From Genesis to Revelation God has been pleading with mankind to get to know Him. Not to know just His works but to be intimate with Him. Paul says in Philippians 3:10(a) "Oh That I may know him, and the power of his resurrection." Above everything else Paul desired to know God. He did not let anything stop him from getting to know the one who loved him so much that He made provision for him to be in covenant relationship with Him. And I wonder is that your desire as well?

Do you want to know God above every other pursuit in your life?

Do you want to know Him before You?

- Obtain that degree
- Build that business
- develop that brand
- love that man

Do you want to know Him? It is my prayer that after you finish reading this chapter on the goodness of God as revealed by His name, you will have an INTENSE desire to know Him. You will experience His goodness daily because you will know His name, which represents His character. That you will continue to pursue knowing God not just for knowledge sake but for intimacy sake.

Because every day that we wake up, is another day where we can experience Him in a new way. There is nothing stale or old about God. His mercies are new every morning because of His great faithfulness. His love never dies because He is love. His knowledge is without end because He is omniscient. Nothing escapes Him because He is omnipresent. Nothing will defeat Him because He is omnipotent. This is the God that we serve, who is asking us to know Him. To know His goodness as revealed by His name.

The Lord is My Shepherd

JEHOVAH-ROHI: יהוה דֹעָה

Psalm 23

Let's look at one of the most memorized passages in the bible, Psalm 23;

The Lord is my shepherd; I shall not want. He maketh me to lie down in green pastures: he leadeth me beside the still waters. He restoreth my soul: he leadeth me in the paths of righteousness for his name's sake. Yea, though I walk through the valley of the shadow of death, I will fear no evil: for thou art with me; thy rod and thy staff they comfort me. Thou preparest a table before me in the presence of mine enemies: thou anointest my head with oil; my cup runneth over. Surely goodness and mercy shall follow me all the days of my life: and I will dwell in the house of the Lord forever.

As a Christian, this passage offers us hope, joy, peace, and contentment because we are in desperate need of a shepherd. The storms of life are raging out of control, and if we do not keep our focus on the one who holds the future we will be lost. The Lord is our Shepherd, and we must rely on Him in all aspects of your life. He loves you with an everlasting love and desires you to rest in Him.

THE LORD IS *MY* SHEPHERD

David did not say the Lord is the shepherd. He said the Lord is my shepherd. He is stating without a shadow of a doubt that God is His. This reminds me of a song by Marvin Sapp called "He Saw the Best in Me" one of the verses says

See he's mine, and I am his,
It doesn't matter what I did,
He only sees me, for who I am,

How comforting it is to know that during a time when people are quick to cut each other off and disown each other, we have a God who wants us and wants us to want Him. The Lord is MY shepherd. A shepherd is one who protects and loves His sheep even to the point of death. In John 10:14-15 Jesus said "I am the good shepherd. I know My own sheep, and they know Me, as the Father knows Me, and I know the Father. I lay down My life for the sheep.

I SHALL NOT WANT

Anything that we need God will provide. Philippians 4:19 says And my God will supply all your needs according to His riches in glory in Christ Jesus. It is not according to whether we deserve it not or whether someone approves or not or whether someone has it or not; but according to God's riches in glory in Christ Jesus. And our God has riches, and is well able to provide for our needs. He says in Psalm 50:10 "for every animal of the forest is Mine, the cattle on a thousand hills." He is Jehovah Jireh God will provide. He will give us everything we need.

- Luke 12:24 "Consider the ravens: they neither sow nor reap, they have neither storehouse nor barn, and yet God feeds them. Of how much more value are you than the birds!
- Psalms 34:10 The young lions suffer want and hunger; but those who seek the LORD lack no good thing.
- Matthew 6:31-32 Therefore do not be anxious, saying, 'What shall we eat?' or 'What shall we drink?' or 'What shall we wear?' For the Gentiles seek after all these things, and your heavenly Father knows that you need them all.

- Philippians 4:19 And my God will supply every need of yours according to his riches in glory in Christ Jesus.
- Romans 8:32 He who did not spare his own Son but gave him up for us all, how will he not also with him graciously give us all things?
- 1 John 3:22 and whatever we ask we receive from him, because we keep his commandments and do what pleases him

HE MAKETH ME TO LIE DOWN IN GREEN PASTURES.

Sometimes God must stop our insanity by making us lie down where we can be fed from His WORD. It is really easy to get caught up in the captivity of activity. We can become so obsessed with doing the things of God that we miss the opportunity to just be with God. We become like Martha in Luke 10:28-42, who was more interested in serving the Lord than in hearing what the Lord had to say. Service in and of itself is not wrong because God has called us to a life of servant hood as exemplified by Jesus Christ. He states in Mark 10:45 For even the Son of Man did not come to be served, but to serve, and to give His life—a ransom for many. But if we are honest with ourselves we are all over the place, because we keep going and going until we burn ourselves out.

We miss deadlines that we had all intentions of meeting. We make promises that we want to keep, but because we miss manage our time, once again we have to cancel and let someone down. Or maybe someone as a need that we feel we have to meet without consulting with God whether or not it is our assignment to meet. We have succumbed to the Martha's mentality instead of the Mary's mentality. Work instead of uninterrupted Worship. God is calling us to rest in Him. Come unto me, all ye that labour and are heavy laden, and I will give you rest. Take my yoke upon you, and learn of me; for I am meek and lowly in heart: and ye shall find rest unto your souls. For my yoke is easy, and my burden is light. Matthew 11:28-30

HE LEADETH ME BESIDE THE STILL WATERS

Still waters represent peace and Jesus is the prince of peace. He leads us and guides us. Not make us or pushes us, because He has given us free will to choose for ourselves which way we should go. Our job is to keep our eyes on Him. Isaiah 26:3 says "You will keep perfectly peaceful the one whose mind remains focused on you, because he remains in you." We are living in time when people are realizing that PEACE is the only answer to the hell we are facing on earth. The problem is that most of us are not turning to the Prince of Peace for the answer instead we are trying to obtain it through our own natural means. Different militant groups are forming and pushing their agenda of arm yourself for battle and get into formation. Now I happen to agree with them. We are to arm ourselves for battle and get in formation. Where we differ is in the type of battle gear we will be using and the formation we will stand in. They want to fight a physical battle with guns, angry words and a mentality that we will get them for what they have done to us; however, the battle will never be won in the physical because it is spiritual in nature. The only way we will ever have peace is to go to the one whose essence is PEACE and that is Jesus Christ Jehovah Shalom. He leads us by the still waters.

HE RESTORETH MY SOUL

Our soul is our mind will and emotions, and because we live in a fallen world; life has a way of creating fragments in our souls where we may have developed a very skewed image of ourselves. An image that is solely based on the opinion of others, not on the designers intended purpose. When God created mankind, He created them in the image of God. He created them male and female to reflect His glory in the earth realm. After the fall of man, God provided us with a savior Jesus Christ, who came to restore us to God's original intent. God, your God, will restore everything you lost; he'll have compassion on you; he'll come back and pick up the pieces from all the places where you were scattered. No matter how far away you end up, God, your God, will get you out of there. Deuteronomy 30:3-4 Message bible. You can become WHOLE by

- **W**alking in victory
- **H**elping others walk in victory
- **O**perating in truthfulness
- **L**istening with understanding
- **E**ntering continued worship

HE LEADETH ME IN THE PATHS OF RIGHTEOUSNESS FOR HIS NAMES SAKE

The name of God shall be great in all the earth. So, we must understand that what we do reflects the greatness of His name. He leads us on the path of righteousness for His name sake Why you may ask? Because God exchanged His righteousness for our unrighteousness when Jesus died on the cross. 2 Corinthians 5:21 says God made him who had no sin to be sin for us, so that in him we might become the righteousness of God. When we walk in our calling as the righteousness of God we do it for His name sake because:

- His name is to be honored- Isaiah 26:13 LORD our God, other lords besides you have ruled over us, but your name alone do we honor.
- His name is to be glorified- Thessalonians 1:12 We pray this so that the name of our Lord Jesus may be glorified in you, and you in him, according to the grace of our God and the Lord Jesus Christ.
- His name is to be praised- Psalm 97:12 Rejoice in the LORD, you who are righteous, and praise his holy name.

So, let's continue to stay on the path of righteousness, and hunger and thirst for righteousness, because God promised we would be filled. Matthew 5:6

YEA, THOUGH I WALK THROUGH THE VALLEY OF THE SHADOW OF DEATH I WILL FEAR NO EVIL BECAUSE YOU ARE WITH ME THY ROD AND THY STAFF THEY COMFORT ME

Thank you Lord for being with us. Thank you for your promise that you will never leave us or forsake us. We are never alone no matter how much it may feel like it. When we cannot feel His presence, we can trust in the truth of His word and the goodness of His heart. Most of the times the thing we fear is only a shadow of what could be (false evidence appearing real). We focus so much on the possible scenarios that we take our eyes of the solution. When we are in situations that may have us a little apprehensive or fearful, we can rest knowing God is with us. We must also remember that the love of God will dispel all shadowy doubt because perfect love cast out fear.

His Rod is used for protection and it stands as a symbol of authority, strength, power and defense. He is an ever-present help in the time of trouble. His STAFF is used to help the us sheep when we get in trouble by pulling us out of situations, and disciplining us when we go in the wrong direction. The use of these tools is comforting even though at times they may not feel like it. God only corrects and disciplines those who belong to Him. My dear child, don't shrug off God's discipline, but don't be crushed by it either. It's the child he loves that he disciplines; the child he embraces, he also corrects. Hebrews 4:6.

THOU PREPAREST A TABLE BEFORE ME IN THE PRESENCE OF MINE ENEMIES. THOU ANOINTEST MY HEAD WITH OIL, MY CUP OVERFLOWS.

Haters cannot stand to see you bless so tell them to take a seat. When we follow the good shepherd in obedience he will anoint us for our assignments, and equip us to sit in the authority of that assignment. We will not have to concern ourselves with those who do not agree with God's choosing because God takes the foolish things of the world to confound the wise. 1 Corinthians 1:7. God chose us and anointed us and that anointing on our lives will overflow into the lives of those assigned to us bringing God glory. Just ask the shepherd boy David. Then Samuel took the horn of oil and anointed him in the midst of his brothers; and the Spirit of the LORD came mightily upon David from that day forward. And Samuel arose and went to Ramah1 Samuel 16:13

SURELY GOODNESS AND MERCY WILL FOLLOW ME ALL THE DAYS OF MY LIFE. I WILL DWELL IN THE HOUSE OF THE LORD FOREVER

We do not have to concern ourselves or worry about who has our back. We are followed by God's goodness and mercy all the days of our lives. It is God's goodness that leads us to repentance. Romans 2:4. It is God's mercies that are new every morning because of His great faithfulness. And because we know Him as our shepherd, our leader, guider, protector, and our savior, we can dwell in His house forever. Psalm 16:11 says You reveal the path of life to me; in Your presence is abundant joy; in Your right hand are eternal pleasures. 1 Thessalonians 4:17 says "Then we who are alive and remain shall be caught up together with them in the clouds, to meet the Lord in the air: and so shall we ever be with the Lord." Come Lord Jesus Come.

THE END OF A THING BUT ALSO THE BEGINNING OF A THING

They will no longer hunger; they will no longer thirst; the sun will no longer strike them,
nor will any heat. For the Lamb who is at the center of the throne will shepherd them;
He will guide them to springs of living waters, and God will wipe away every tear from their eyes. Revelation 7:16-17

As we **end** this chapter on Psalm 23, I pray that you have a greater love for the goodness of God as reveled in His name Jehovah Rohi-The Lord is my Shepherd. Because when all is said and done, we will forever be with our good shepherd. The one who laid down His life, so we might live. I also pray that you will **begin** your own quest of getting to know God by His other names as revealed in the scriptures. I promise you, you will never be the same.

Because the Lord is my Shepherd, I have everything I need.
He knows my heart so intimately, I can trust in Him to lead.
This truth is fulfilled in Jesus Christ, He is Jehovah Rohi.
He teaches and guides and fills me with joy, my Shepherd He'll always be. (Kristy Caffull)

Rayshoun Chambers

Rayshoun Chambers has successfully held senior leadership positions within best-in-class organizations, including First Data, Elavon, and WorldPay U.S. As the Founder, CEO of RAC Venture Group, LLC. Her company brings Six Sigma methodologies to small companies and corporations resulting in project and program movement from concept to cash flow. As an Author, payments professional, fierce coach, proud mom, lover of Christ and loyal friend, she fashions herself a lifetime student. The drive she garnered over the years allow her to push past NO's for the YES just on the other side. Rayshoun has recently become increasingly sought after for speaking engagements, collaborations and professional projects – the likes of which she cheerfully participates in if the alignment is right.

You can follow her on Twitter @RayshounC,
www.facebook.com/racwrites,
https://www.linkedin.com/in/rayshounchambers/

"Surviving" From the Sidelines

It's unusually quiet today, but I rather enjoy this time to myself. I like these moments with my coffee, my notepad and God. I used to tell myself this was the time to speak to Him. It was years before I realized it was really the time that He speaks to me. Now before you go to thinking that I must be crazy and need some sort of medical assistance, not in the sense of an audible voice, like the ones we hear speaking to us every day, but I always found it interesting that God found a way to speak to me in a voice that I've heard all of my life- often times through my own voice. I would actually go to Him with a problem, something I considered a major concern, and from there I would just start talking to myself in the mirror. My facial expressions were always interesting to me, the ones I made with certain words, but nonetheless I would do it. Over time it became therapeutic. It's been a long time since I found myself standing here like this ...again in front of the mirror, talking until something came out of my mouth that made sense. But this time it was different.

****

"Rayshoun, we are calling from the oncology department at Duke Medical Hospital, can you hear me ok? We have your mother here. We have found cancer. Several tumors, and a massive blood clot and need to begin a rigorous treatment plan for her. She will need chemotherapy and radiation treatment Monday through Friday. We're calling you because she is not able to speak to you directly right now. She is emotional about her ability to transport herself to and from treatments. Are you aware that our facility is an hour and 15 minutes away from her residence?

No ma'am, but ok. Well you seem to be taking this much better than we thought, because we need to start this treatment promptly, by any chance would you be able to get her to her appointments daily?... Ma'am there's no question as to whether or not she and I will be there, please proceed forward with scheduling whatever procedures you need to for my mom and I'll meet you in person next week. "

****

L-U-N-G C-A-N-C-E-R. I softly and quietly spelled those letters over and over, looking myself in the mirror of my hotel room. Tears where streaming down my face as if they were part of some mystical waterfall. I mean, personally could not control the flow of them- but imagined an angel swiftly descending down to catch them and transporting them back to God for me ... and somehow though I did not have the words today, I knew the resolution was underway in God's lab from the content of my tears.

That was a tough call to get, some six and a half seven hours away on business, about the woman who brought you into the world. I don't even know if people would be honest about the rushing feeling of emotions you experience when you are one the sidelines watching someone you love prepare for the match-up of their life. I honestly believed there were no real comforting words I could share... I mean could cover her with prayer, yes. I could tell her that by His Stripes she is healed, yes. But what could I authentically tell her that would give her any degree of comfort we need in the natural? That day I came back to her house in Rocky Mount, NC; I simply gave her hug and said **"I will be with you every day"** and I thanked God for the ability to tell her that and in that very moment - I could sense both mom and me gained some comfort.

I remember early on the treatment process, we dropped my son off at Day Care and headed on up the road to the treatment center. I rather enjoy the rides up the road to Raleigh- just some mommy and me time to reflect, doing sing-a-longs (yeppers, mom always wanted to sing-a-long to Mary J. Blige) and of the course occasional stop for some Cajun boiled peanuts. We did not stop every day, but definitely mentioned them each time we passed the exit. I went to speak with the caseworker while mom got settled in for treatment. Let me tell you something, it has always been hard for me to ask others for help - always - and this was no different. In fact it was even more difficult, because we had much, much more on the line. It is amazing the questions you have to answer, the paperwork you need to supply, all of the things that are required from a patient just to get a gas card to even make it to treatments. Given mom's appointment hours and location, working was not something I was going to be able to do for a while; not to mention having an SUV, $95/week for gas, things were going to be catching up with us real soon. However, when your other option is $120 one-way = $240/day for other transport options, you realize quickly how blessed you are; so off to the caseworker I went, to try and get support for mom and me during this process. After I met with the case worker I went back downstairs to check on mama bear, I when the nurse came over she was requesting her to turn up the frequency of her chemo-IV drip. I could see her foot rocking and saw her looking at the clock. It was more than clear mama bear wanted to jet outta that facility in time enough for me to get my son from Day Care. She didn't want me to leave, go get him and come back to pick her up. Like we had done the day prior. Aside from the 3hr drive that would be for me (totaling 6 hrs in one day) she didn't want to burn the gas, so she worried that nurse until her meds were coming down at warp speed. I left the hospital that day knowing I was going to pray for peace with my next decision.

******

I called the Daycare and let them know my son would not be returning. Together my son and I prepared his pre-school kit, complete with charts, books, alphabets, markers, iPad the works and of course his red backpack, we thought of everything, even the action figures and trains for 'break time'. That became the new routine. Pack Up the kid, get mama bear and we were off to slay the day as a family, bound to win with God. On breaks (basically when the hospital got too cold to sit still) we would go to the courtyard and sit amongst the trees. Sometimes I would blow bubbles and Cameron would chase them so hard with undisputed determination. In my head I would imagine each one held the cure for a different type of cancer, and when he caught one, I always breathed a slight sigh of relief. Children are so pure at heart, I have no idea if I'm right or wrong with my imagination in the courtyard... because honestly only God knows what the future holds. There was a time when I would wake more uncertain than I was the day before. I would go to bed at night more uncertain than I was that morning...but I began to de-construct Mathew 6:31-33 and knowing that God already truly knows everything single thing I could desire to bring to Him in prayer only made me that much more committed to do so. Opening myself up to the obedience and faithfulness is what it was going to require to make sure I remained strong enough to survive from the sidelines.

****

Afternoon naps are the best! Well, usually unless you wake up to the sound of a lawnmower hacking away at the grass outside. Normally, something like this would send me into an area of frustration you could liken to a kid having to share their favorite toy. I adore my rest. But this day I looked out the window and popped to my feet. It is Brother Farmer, from St. John AMEZ Methodist church, mama bears church home! Praise the Lord! The grass was getting taller every week and that was a discretionary expense that we could not swing during this time. Knowing how important mama bear's house is to her, having him coming over to cut the grass during her treatment was mega helpful. We were getting loved on from so many places. Pastor Bradshaw came over and prayed and left a gift card and such, and our friend Heather Owens brought a gas card and some yummy treats. We were surrounded by love. The enemy did not want me to give God praise for the people He sent to be a blessing to us. Nope, the enemy was quite pleased with the thoughts I had about the GoFundme Page with only 2 donations, or the phone calls that seemed to stop coming in, as if they had already mentally buried my mother. Not just her phone, but my phone as well. It was almost as if we had faded in to a forgotten community, the place you go when no one knows how to address your pain. The land they cast you to when they forget you are still a person, and that laughter still helps heal the spirit. He wanted me to be consumed with those negative toxins of the mind. But God kept me and because of that I could wake up and proclaim "I let go of my anger so I can see clearly". "I am ready for the steps God will order today". But my daily affirmation was a decision to set me on the path, to walk actively, daily with God, and I must say I rather enjoy His Company. The road ahead was long, the days were difficult but no longer **uncertain** or anxiety laden.

****

"Hey Ray, come here for second". Being the excitable type person my mother is, I wasn't used to this calm voice when she was in a different room. So I cautiously approached and with good cause; when I walked into her doorway she was taking down her cornrows style braids. That was a style she wore her shoulder length hair whenever she wore one of her glamorous wigs. Only this time the full cornrow was on her hair comb. Her hair was falling out at a rapid speed, I could clearly see a large bald area at the top of her head. She told me that was from the cornrows she had tried to undo just moments before. *"Awh mimah, I see it babe"*...she looked up at me from her seated position and said *"Welp baby girl, mimah's head is about to be as butt-naked as a chicken"*... and that is when I knew the fight was on and she had no plans to lose. She went ahead that day and got rid of all the rest of her hair that was hanging on, waiting for its day to fallout. She took a stand and said she was going to release that hair - that day! Later that

evening, Cameron saw her walking down the hallway and said *"Hey Mimah! You look sooooo handsome"*... and she gave him such a big hug. It's funny how 3-year olds say the most honest things! But he was so proud of his Mimah that day, and well, as for me... I was so proud of them both.

****

I had been a victim of identity theft, nearly black balled from my career industry. My oldest brother Lord Michael had suffered a stroke not even a good 7 months before mom received the stage 3 Lung Cancer diagnosis. I would be dishonest if I did not say I wondered what message God was sending to me. I threw every ounce of support I knew how to at the situation. I mean, I know for sure there were people in the world going through more than I was at that point in time. But I also knew what was important was for me to continue to tap into what was meant for ME to gather. My dad, Phil Chambers always told me that in life, the things we experience are meant to be a lesson or a blessing; so I knew it was for me to continue this walk with God, not as a speck on a map praying to someone in the great distance. But rather as a true sideline coach, yelling to go harder, keep pushing and more importantly, DON'T QUIT. I had been going about this whole "surviving" thing the wrong way! I needed to invite God INTO MY SITUATION. No trick cameras and no make-up. Not to keep praying for Him to be some sort of long distance Angel investor. But for Him to be front and center; with me daily- all day- each day. Those nights when my mom's violent coughs would wake me; that's when I prayed myself back to sleep and I would have His hand physically upon me as I thanked Him for being so masterful in my life. For being my 'everything'- I learned what it meant to experience God's presence in my life. You have to admit there is a fantastic comfort in knowing your life, your thoughts and things around you are a complete and utter mess, yet you can invite God in without having to say "Please excuse the house" and what's more?? He will even help us **clean it up!**

******

I know when I call my dad he can hear the excitement in my voice as I continue to look at things with my *new eyes*. I know that God is my overseer and He truly was my overseer during my mother's lung cancer treatments. I was so blind walking into that battle with her, I have always been called her rock! I have always had her back! Yet this battle was one of which I had no natural ammunition. Trade places with me for a moment and just image, every question, having an answer. Every request, you are there in a blink of an eye, and then one day you get that call, only this time you are not trouble shooting an Internet error message. You are not making a stop to pick up some seasoned meat from the store or even taking the trash out for her; Nope, this time you are being confronted with an issue that a mere swipe of a debit card cannot resolve. As I stood in that hotel room mirror, I knew that the enemy wanted to have me. "Little Miss Optimistic", I could literally see the clouds of doubt attempt to move in and cause an overcast on the sun rays of blessings that God had on the roadmap for me. You know that voice that tries to ask you things like "how you gonna pay your car note? What about your consulting contract? What are you going to do?" but I remember my Pastor Michael Cloer spoke about how we tend to be so focused on **the blessing that we forget about the Bless-or.** I knew in that moment I did not want to be that person.

But I started to grow up in my walk, I started to share more about what sort of spiritual support I needed, started doing my part, and as always God had the rest. I had been attending Englewood Baptist Church for a year but had not joined a bible fellowship group. One day I got a call from Julie Green and made the personal decision to start growing up in my church here in NC. That has been part of my growth process and is very necessary in order to for any of us to truly grow; we have to study. There were many people, meetings, prayers and all that continue to contribute to my growth, both my mother and brother's restoration and my journey.

Praise, glory and thanks be to God for the cancer remission for my mother. She is a cancer conqueror, a warrior for Christ, a flawed being, a tough-skinned Grandma and the best mom she has been equipped to be. Thank God for the trials, thank God for the tribulations and most of all thank God for the lessons and to God be the glory for the blessings.

Points of Power for the Survivors on the Sideline:

- Meditation is so important, if you don't currently meditate, please start; there are many resources but commit to start small 10-15 mins increments

- Daily affirmations work!

- Take care of your temple, mind what you consume. Read your product packages in food and watch your sodium and sugar levels

- Not just food but all consumption to include media consumption. Facebook, Twitter and other social media and Television exposure. Ensure they are things that uplift you.

- Read, read, read - stay plugged in and keep your brain active

- Laugh, laugh, laugh - if it has been more than 24hours since your last laugh go now and find something humorous

- Pray, pray, pray - speak to Him your way. With your true heart. Just because we know someone doesn't mean we don't miss them! When we are apart from Him, he misses us too.

Those are just a few of the things I began to do consistently, and note that is the entire point of it all; **being consistent.** When I did those things I became more aware of His presence in my life daily. I began to sense his presence during those stressful times when our funding requests were not being processed timely to get us the support we needed to get my mom to treatment. I started to notice more things that I would have missed otherwise; all those times my son was inquiring about how his Grandma was doing and if she needed to keep seeing 'those doctors' as he called them. I would not have been able to give him my true heartfelt honest answer, when I held his hands in mine… we placed our foreheads together and raised prayers to God for Grandma. You have no idea the joy that filled my heart to hear him say *"Dear God, this prayer is for Grandma, we love her, we love You, we trust you, Amen."* My God! How simple children make the things we adults have over complicated for years. I am not biblical scholar, and I am actually okay with that. I am a royal daughter of the King and he knows not only my heart but my next actions. I am grateful for His love and His love is for **you too.** Often times, and rightfully so, there is a major focus on the person with the illness, fighting that daily battle one moment at a time. As a sideline player, I know personally that it is a very tough position to maintain. Like the patient, you are drafted in to the role and before you know it, its game time. It's extremely hard to watch someone you love struggle with something that you cannot help them resolve. There are countless hours of sleep you will not get back. There are tears you will cry that you never knew you had inside. There will be loneliness, in part from friends or people whose lives continue as they were before your life changed forever and also because you will mourn the level of engagement you had with your loved one before the illness got a foothold in their life. The reality will seem grim no matter how optimistic you are because grief occurs not just after a loss, but begins with the impact of impending loss. But there is JOY. Joy in knowing we serve a God of purpose, restoration, grace and mercy. A joy in knowing that even if the outcome does not match the prayers you sent to heaven, the outcome will be for your good. The outcome will strengthen you. That even during a time of extreme darkness, our Lord is with us and surely goodness and mercy shall follow us all the days of our life, and we will dwell in the house of the Lord forever.

I Dedicate

Glory to God for being my ever-after, my protector and provider. To my mother, Joanne Smaw-Asomugha, my father Phil Chambers, siblings Lord Michael Chambers, John Gaines and Corey Chambers, I love you and am blessed by you. To my son - God has already gifted you with so much, Cameron Lewis Chambers, and I am proud of you. Continue to witness and show people of all ages the wonders that come from having a personal relationship with Him. To my Bible Fellowship Sisters at Englewood Baptist Church, led by Regina Green and Julie Green thank you so much, I love you all.

Rayshoun Chambers

Betty Speaks

BETTY SPEAKS is the Executive Director at "STRAP EM UP BOOT CAMP" and the founder of "BETTY SPEAKS "IT". A Certified Life Coach, Betty is an *Intentional Transformation Storyteller*.

She is an Army Veteran, Ambassador to The Veteran Woman LLC., a Global Network Virtual Marketer and Entrepreneur, 5x Best Selling Author, Ordained Pastor, Jesus Woman at Godheads Ministry, Ambassador to the Pink Pulpit Crusade International and a Designated Mastery Story Teller.

Betty holds a Bachelor of Science in Business Management from the University of Maryland. She received 5 Outstanding Businesswoman of The Year awards from the American Business Women's Association.

Betty speaks passion and life's calling is to help others not just survive, but thrive in the face of chances, challenges or changes.

DISCIPLINE, DETERMINATION, AND BRAVERY

*"An authentic leader holds on to His peace
while enduring a process.
An authentic leader takes the required actions as
situations comes about, an authentic leader,
never forgets that through their process
they must remain at peace.
An authentic leader, remains inspired from the
core of their heart.
An authentic leader, leads us into stillness,
for our very own safety and protection."*
Betty Speaks

Personal life experiences, allowed me to be mindful that being a leader takes discipline, determination, and bravery. Although to some being a leader can bring about great success, it can come at the price of experiencing un wanted judgement or challenging growth. The Bible communicates to us of so many pleasing leaders and just how God blessed each of them for their endeavors. For the most part, there are several verses and Scriptures that God spoke on to encourage those of us who choose to step forward and lead as leaders should lead. Such as; Hebrews 13:7 NIV *Remember your leaders who spoke the word of God to you. Consider the outcome of their way of life and imitate their fate.*

DISCIPLINE

The Lord as our shepherd guides or leads us to a path of stillness, restoration and revelation. Meditation in a time of peace while in His presence only! Not relying on the voices of others but His alone. I have been exposed to dreadful environments that I do not wish upon no one. I use this time of stillness (while in pain, especially as a leader), to reflect plus grow closer to Jesus and to hide more of His word into my heart! As I recall the picture of a shepherd carrying one of his sheep, I am reminded just how much I love that picture of the him carrying his sheep around his neck. I also love story behind the picture that so many are unaware of. You see, the shepherd loved and cared for his sheep as carefully and tenderly as a father loves and cares for his children. He always made sure that his flock was well cared for. Like a good leader, the Shepherd, would also walk ahead of the sheep to show them a new trail to new pastures, then often he would walk behind, making sure that no straggler was separated from the flock. I also learned that often when the grass was dry and parched from the heat of the summer, the sheep would be prone to mosey, drifting to the cool of the wooden craving greener meadows. Nonetheless, the shepherd would cautiously keep them away for he knew that the woodland was panic-stricken by the mountain lions that found the sheep easy prey and it was filled with crevices that the sheep would fall into and get wounded. At times this was difficult, for the sheep did not understand why the temptation of the forest was such a danger.

Nevertheless, he remained firm in spite of their whining, mindful that the temptation of green meadows is often a verdict of death rather than a giver of life.

If you are striving to be a discipline leader or if you need inspiration along the way, these Bible verses about leadership discipline are essential! One of my favorites is Proverbs 23:12 ASV *Apply your heart to discipline And your ears to words of knowledge.*

Likewise, I believe that leaders are good at many things, tolerance, however, is naturally not one of them. In a society that is quickly getting use to the "now effect" we are always wanting things a lot sooner, in the military they have the cliché "hurry up and wait." Which means that nothing has a time limit or value on it. It happens Also, we want things to more improved, much better, etc. while a certain kind of process can be a boring thing, whether it's the "sparkler of death" on one's processor, or the foreseeable line time at Disney World, leaders are constantly in a place of process. According to His word process is all around us, and while we can learn to enjoy it, being mindful of it is the first step of finding peace. (John 16:33). It took a process of peace for the shepherd to nurse his intentional wounded lamb back to entrusting him and his leadership.

The actual purpose of such discipline should not as cruel as one would think. It should be done with love in mind. As in the moral of the picture of the Shepherd with the sheep around his neck. You see, the shepherd intentionally broke the sheep's leg as to discipline him for going astray, not being an obedient lamb or being defiant. The Shepherd being a good leader disciplined his lamb out of love as it is written in Galatians 6:1 *we are told to restore our fallen brother in a spirit of gentleness, because we also could be tempted and fall. Just remind yourself that it could happen to you. We are all vulnerable.*

Likewise, all discipline of sin should be done to restore a one's contentment or their enjoyment. One who obviously commits a sin or a dishonorable act as the sheep was to his shepherd which resulted into a broken leg leading the sheep to lose his joy and his fullness as a sheep, as a result the sheep like us cannot be restored from our sin until there is a period of discipline.

Yet, that discipline leader or shepherd will lead to peace in the process of rest in accordance to Proverbs 29:17 ASV, **correct** *thy son, and he will give thee rest; Yea, he will give delight unto thy soul.*

DETERMINATION

What I love about one of my younger brothers (Pastor John H. Hinson), is that he wholeheartedly displays his ability to be a real leader who is ordinary with extraordinary determination. Like the shepherd, he leads with comprehension of other being and involve them to help in accomplishing a task. This requires good characteristics, comparable skills, integrity, dedication of purpose, selflessness, knowledge plus determination not to accept disappointments.

Also, being in leadership, requires one's presence around, involved plus having relationships with others. Whether you carry the title of a shepherd or not, if you love others and care about their outcome in life, then you are a good shepherd. Like my brother's heart, our heart as shepherds is to guide and care for folks as they go through their own process. Sometimes that's easier said than done. One will go through times where they feel not only proud but furious, upset, hopeful, appreciative and weary all in the same individuals. It's normal to feel and direct those emotions, but what isn't normal is to intemperance the person when you're tired of their current emotion impact on your leadership. That's part of the process, enjoy it.

Process isn't about putting a pause on our dreams, it's about learning to recognize the growth attached to it. Next time you find yourself frustrated with the process, remind yourself the pain point you feel is the proof that growth is happening.

Peacefully, a leader moves things onward one opportunity at a time. This is exactly what a shepherd does with his sheep's. He here hears Difficulties and projects, they are all a gift. Locating that sweet spot where you're slightly challenged yet not completely overwhelmed, one can continue to grow your gifts and talents and turn them into an expression of your Kingdom assignment in excellence.

Therefore, and personally a leader not a person, put, themselves in an area, a process. Ideally, a process that is constantly changing. Constantly growing and developing them for success. Such a leader keeps showing up to the places that matter (their righteousness, in relationships and in personal reflection) and learn to love the process you are in peacefully.

BRAVERY

Yes, even a female leader can be still and display bravery as it is written! 1 Co 16:13, Paul commands the Corinthians to "be brave" (NKJV).

Bravery means knowing that Christ is God.
Robert Murray McCheyne quotes, *"When Christ delays to help His saints now, you think this is a great mystery, you cannot explain it; but Jesus sees the end from the beginning. Be still, and know that Christ is God"*

Bravery By being Still

Psalm 46:10-11 *"Be still, and know that I am God! I will be honored by every nation. I will be honored throughout the world." The LORD of Heaven's Armies is here among us; the God of Israel is our fortress.*

Bravery By Perseverance

Psalm 23:4 *Even when I must walk through the darkest valley, I fear no danger, for you are with me; your rod and your staff reassure me.*

Bravery while fighting

Exodus 14:14 *"The LORD will fight for you while you keep still."*

Bravery is being still by shutting of social media
Joshua 1:8 *This law scroll must not leave your lips! You must memorize it day and night, so you can carefully obey all that is written in it. Then you will prosper and be successful.*

Bravery will find peace because if we are always busy doing other things. We need to cease and allow Christ to give us a peace that the no one can't offer.

Colossians 3:15 Let the peace of the Messiah also rule in your hearts, to which you were called in one body, and be thankful.

Philippians 4:7 And the peace of God that surpasses all understanding will guard your hearts and minds in Christ Jesus.

Bravery while being still in His presence brings comfort;
Fear not, for I am with you; be not dismayed, for I am your God; I will strengthen you, I will help you, I will uphold you with my righteous right hand. Behold, all who are incensed against you shall be put to shame and confounded; those who strive against you shall be as nothing and shall perish. You shall seek those who contend with you, but you shall not find them; those who war against you shall be as nothing at all. For I, the L\ORD your God, hold your right hand; it is I who say to you, "Fear not, I am the one who helps you." Isaiah 41 10-13

Bravery in the mist of your storm

And when he got into the boat, his disciples followed him. And behold, there arose a great storm on the sea, so that the boat was being swamped by the waves; but he was asleep. And they went and woke him, saying, "Save us, Lord; we are perishing." And he said to them, "Why are you afraid, O you of little faith?" Then he rose and rebuked the winds and the sea, and there was a great calm. And the men marvelled, saying, "What sort of man is this, that even winds and sea obey him?" Matthew8 23-27

Bravery to the Most High
Psalm 91-116 *"He who dwells in the shelter of the Most High will abide in the shadow of the Almighty. I will say to the LORD, "My refuge and my fortress, my God, in whom I trust." For he will deliver you from the snare of the fowler and from the deadly pestilence. He will cover you with his pinions, and under his wings you will find refuge; his faithfulness is a shield and buckler. You will not fear the terror of the night, nor the arrow that flies by day"*

Bravery is a reminder that there is peace in the process during times when you have fearful and uneasy feelings that are furious within you like a ferocious storm, do as Jesus did. Quiet those feelings by saying, "Peace, be still." Once you need strength and help, let go and rest in God, your refuge. *"Be still and know that I am God."*

Still waters bring discipline, determination, and bravery as there is peace in the process of its dwellings that is driven from staying the word and presence our Lord.

I Dedicate

I give an honor to God for His presence in my life. I honor my younger brother whom I witness struggling from his incubator at birth, being reborn by giving his life to Christ; and now ordained as a Pastor a Godlike Shepherd to his sheep – Pastor John H Hinson III, PhD. His mantra is "In peace I will lie down and sleep, for you alone, Lord, make me dwell in safety.
"Psalm 4:8"!

Betty Speaks

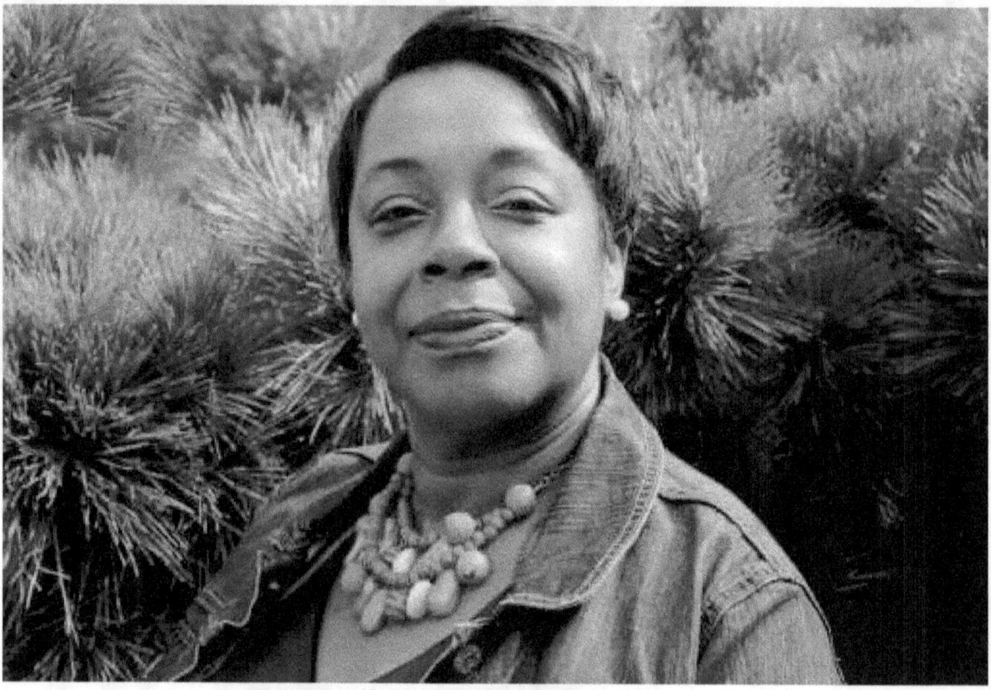

Dr. Marilyn "M.E." Porter
Founder and Senior Publisher

www.thescatterbrainedgenius.com/publishing

www.ingramcontent.com/pod-product-compliance
Lightning Source LLC
Chambersburg PA
CBHW070551300426
44113CB00011B/1864